Sports Illustrated KIDS

STARS OF SPORTS

SABRINA IONESCU

RISING BASKETBALL STAR

by *Matt Chandler*

CAPSTONE PRESS
a capstone imprint

Published by Capstone Press, an imprint of Capstone
1710 Roe Crest Drive, North Mankato, Minnesota 56003
capstonepub.com

Library of Congress Cataloging-in-Publication Data
Names: Chandler, Matt, author. Title: Sabrina Ionescu : rising basketball star / by Matt Chandler.
Description: North Mankato, Minnesota : Capstone Press, 2022. | Series: Sports illustrated kids stars of sports | Includes bibliographical references and index. | Audience: Ages 8-11 | Audience: Grades 4-6 |
Summary: "Around three years old, Sabrina Ionescu picked up a basketball. While she had natural talent, Ionescu worked hard. In middle school there weren't enough players for a girls' basketball team. Ionescu wasn't allowed on the boys' team, but she didn't give up. Instead, she recruited enough girls to make a team. Learn about how Ionescu became the first overall pick in the 2020 WNBA draft and the player she is today"—Provided by publisher.
Identifiers: LCCN 2021033324 (print) | LCCN 2021033325 (ebook) | ISBN 9781663983626 (hardcover) | ISBN 9781666323368 (paperback) | ISBN 9781666323375 (pdf) | ISBN 9781666323399 (kindle edition)
Subjects: LCSH: Ionescu, Sabrina, 1997-—Juvenile literature. | Women basketball players—United States—Biography—Juvenile literature. Classification: LCC GV884.I66 C53 2022 (print) | LCC GV884.I66 (ebook) | DDC 796.323092 [B]—dc23
LC record available at https://lccn.loc.gov/2021033324
LC ebook record available at https://lccn.loc.gov/2021033325

Editorial Credits
Editor: Christianne Jones; Designer: Bobbie Nuytten; Media Researcher: Morgan Walters; Production Specialist: Laura Manthe

Image Credits
Associated Press: Adam Hunger, 28, Andy Nelson/The Register-Guard, 21, Phelan M. Ebenhack, 26, 27; Getty Images: MediaNews Group/The Mercury News via Getty Images, 11, MediaNews Group/The Mercury News via Getty Images, 15, 16; Newscom: Cody Glenn/Icon Sportswire DMD, Cover, 5, Larry C. Lawson/Cal Sport Media, 9, Naoki Nishimura/AFLO SPORT, 23, Rich Graessle/Icon Sportswire CGV, 13, Robin Alam/Icon Sportswire 164, 19, Thurman James/Cal Sport Media, 4, ylan Stewart/Image of Sport, 25; Shutterstock: Girts Ragelis, 1, Mohammad-amin asareh, 7

Source Notes
Page 8, "And now I use...," Sabrina Ionescu, "The Legend of Sabrina Ionescu," *ESPN*, March 16, 2020, https://www.espn.com/espn/feature/story/_/id/28878754/the-legend-sabrina-ionescu, Accessed June 24, 2021.
Page 10, "My middle school...," Sabrina Ionescu, "Her middle school said to play with dolls. She set an NCAA triple-double record instead." *The Washington Post,* February 4, 2019, https://www.washingtonpost.com/sports/2019/02/04/her-middle-school-said-play-with-dolls-she-set-an-ncaa-triple-double-record-instead/, Accessed June 24, 2021.
Page 12, "I wish I could...," Sabrina Ionescu, "Her middle school said to play with dolls. She set an NCAA triple-double record instead." *The Washington Post,* February 4, 2019, https://www.washingtonpost.com/sports/2019/02/04/her-middle-school-said-play-with-dolls-she-set-an-ncaa-triple-double-record-instead/, Accessed June 24, 2021.
Page 14, "Sabrina had her...," Kelly Sopak, "The Legend of Sabrina Ionescu," *ESPN*, March 16, 2020, https://www.espn.com/espn/feature/story/_/id/28878754/the-legend-sabrina-ionescu, Accessed June 24, 2021.
Page 14, "Yeah, she doesn't miss...," Eddy Ionescu, "The Legend of Sabrina Ionescu," *ESPN*, March 16, 2020, https://www.espn.com/espn/feature/story/_/id/28878754/the-legend-sabrina-ionescu, Accessed June 24, 2021.

TABLE OF CONTENTS

Words in **BOLD** are in the glossary.

RECORD SETTER

On February 24, 2020, the Oregon Ducks were leading the Stanford Cardinals by 18 points late in the third quarter. Basketball fans around the country were watching to see if Oregon senior Sabrina Ionescu could set a new record. In NCAA Division I basketball history, no player had ever scored 2,000 points and had 1,000 assists and 1,000 rebounds. Ionescu was one rebound away from making history.

》》》 Ionescu drives to the basket with the ball on February 24, 2020.

With the Cardinal on offense, Ionescu positioned herself under the basket. Cardinal guard Hannah Jump took a pass and launched a three-point shot. Her shot missed and went straight into Ionescu's hands. She had done it! The Ducks went on to win the game, 74–66. Oregon finished the 2019–20 season with a record of 31–2 thanks to the play of their record-setting senior.

>>> Ionescu celebrates with her teammates after breaking the NCAA basketball record and winning the game against Stanford.

CHAPTER ONE

CALIFORNIA TWIN

Sabrina Ionescu was born in Walnut Creek, California, on December 6, 1997. Her parents are immigrants from Romania. She also has a twin brother, Eddy, who shares her love for basketball. Sabrina and Eddy have an older brother, Andrei.

Sabrina and Eddy developed their love for the sport growing up. They often went to a park near their home and spent day after day playing basketball. They practiced nonstop. They played pickup games. They challenged players to games of H-O-R-S-E. They sometimes played against adults. The many hours spent on the courts helped Ionescu build her skills.

>>> Walnut Creek, California, is in the San Francisco Bay area. It is surrounded by hills and forested areas.

FACT

Ionescu speaks English and Romanian. She and her brother used to talk to each other in Romanian on the basketball court. It kept their opponents from knowing what the twins were going to do.

BROTHERLY LOVE

Though she has two brothers, Ionescu is extra close with her twin. They are self-described best friends. He has been her biggest fan throughout her life.

Ionescu says both of her brothers played hard against her. Eddy never took it easy on his sister on the basketball court. Eddy said many of their games ended with one of them having a busted lip or a nosebleed!

Today, Ionescu is known for being a strong player with her left hand. She told a story of Eddy once teasing her about how he was better with his left hand than she was. Ionescu forced herself to play with only her left hand for several days. Her determination to beat her brother helped shape her game today. "And now I use my left hand more than my right," she said.

FACT

Eddy transferred to the University of Oregon before his sister's junior year and shared an apartment with her.

>>> Ionescu shows her ability to play with her left hand in a 2019 game.

CHAPTER TWO
A GIRL WITHOUT A TEAM

By the time she reached middle school, Ionescu had fallen in love with the game. She was excited to play on her middle school team. Then she got the bad news: There was no basketball team for girls. Ionescu asked about playing on the boys' team. "My middle school said I should be playing with dolls," she said in a 2019 interview.

Sabrina didn't give up. She asked other girls if they wanted to form a team to play basketball. She also forced her way into playing with the boys. She would attend Eddy's games and bring her sneakers with her. She hoped they would be short a player and she could get in the game. Sometimes, it worked.

〉〉〉 Ionescu's focus on basketball continued into her high school years.

FACT

Ionescu is ambidextrous. That means she can do things equally as well with her left hand or her right hand.

FOLLOWING HER DREAMS

Even after being told to go play with dolls, Ionescu never quit. When she was 12 years old, she wrote a speech. It was about her love of basketball. She said she was going to keep working to one day become a WNBA player.

It would have been easy for Ionescu to give up. Instead, she worked harder to make her dreams come true. Today, the former number-one WNBA Draft pick is a professional basketball player. But she never forgot what it was like to be told to play with dolls instead of following her dream. "I wish I could go back and just tell those people they had made a mistake," she said.

》》》 Ionescu's determination to play her best is apparent in every game.

CHAPTER THREE

HIGH SCHOOL STAR

Ionescu made her high school varsity team in her first year, but she wasn't a starter. Her high school coach said Ionescu sat the bench for the first half of her freshman year. "Sabrina had her share of failures . . . " said her coach, Kelly Sopak.

Eddy told a story of a **playoff game** in Sabrina's freshman year where the failure and determination came together. With 2.6 seconds left in the game, Ionescu stood at the free throw line. She had a chance to tie or even win the game for her team. She missed the free throw. She was heartbroken. She cried. And then, according to Eddy, she went straight to the gym and shot free throws for hours. "Yeah, she doesn't miss free throws very often anymore," he said.

>>> Ionescu congratulates a player on the other team after a 2015 loss by her high school team.

>>> Teammates carry Ionescu after winning the open division semifinal game in 2016.

GROWTH IN HER GAME

Once she became a starter, Ionescu quickly became a superstar. Tall players might be great rebounders. Quick players can rack up a lot of assists. Players with a perfect shot score many points. Ionescu could do all three. She said the balance in her game came from playing mostly against boys growing up. They didn't want to pass her the ball, so she learned to rebound.

In sixth grade, she played against much taller players on the eighth grade team. That made shooting difficult, so she learned to be a great passer. Hundreds of hours on the court with her brother made her a great shooter. Ionescu was a complete player. In her three seasons as a starter, Miramonte High School never won less than 30 games. **Scouts** began to take notice. Ionescu's play would soon make her one of the highest rated basketball **recruits** in the nation.

CHAPTER FOUR
COLLEGE BALLER

Many high school athletes choose their college early. Ionescu was different. She couldn't decide where she wanted to go. She was recruited by many great colleges. Of all the players in the 2016 McDonald's All American Game, Ionescu was the only one who had not yet chosen her college. Finally, in June, she decided she was going to be an Oregon Duck.

Ionescu didn't even tell Oregon basketball coach Kelly Graves she was coming. She just arrived at the school and went straight to the gym to let him know. The next day she began her college career.

>>> After joining the Ducks, Ionescu had many celebratory moments with Kelly Graves (left) and her teammates.

READY FOR THE PROS

After her junior year at Oregon, Ionescu was eligible for the WNBA Draft. Many experts expected her to be chosen number one. Ionescu shocked basketball fans everywhere when she announced she was going to stay at Oregon and finish her college career. Ionescu wanted a shot to win a national championship. She was willing to risk injury and miss out on the WNBA for a chance to help the Ducks win it all.

In her senior year, Ionescu led the Ducks to a record of 31–2. The team had an opportunity to bring a national title to Oregon. Then the **COVID-19 pandemic** hit. The NCAA canceled the tournament.

Ionescu set records and won every major award her senior season. It was time for her to make her dream come true. She was ready for the WNBA!

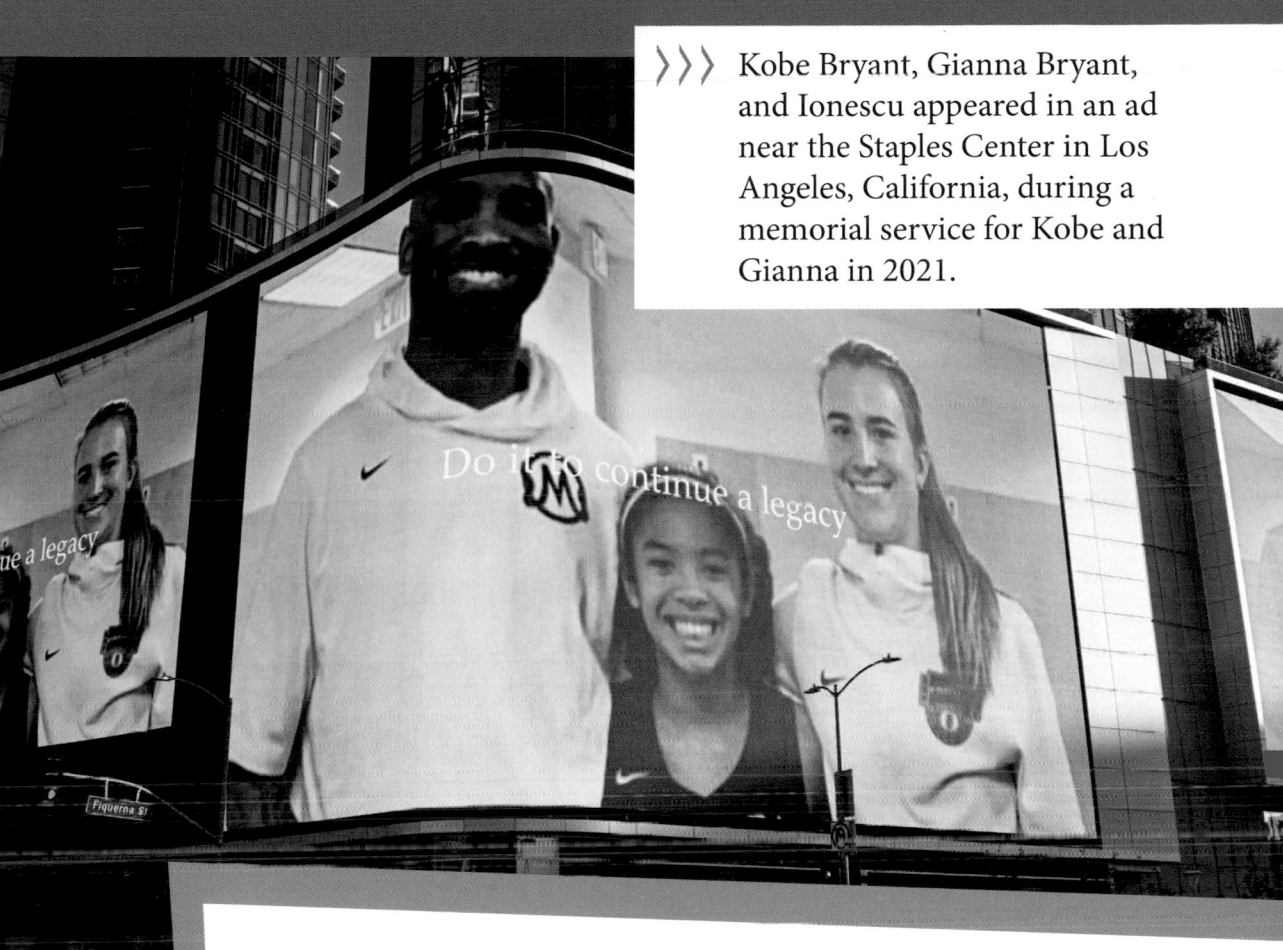

Friendship with Kobe Bryant

On January 11, 2019, the Ducks were playing a game against the University of Southern California Trojans. Former Los Angeles Lakers superstar Kobe Bryant attended the game. Bryant spoke to the team and made a connection with Ionescu. He became her **mentor**. He would text or call her after big games. She worked out with Bryant and his daughter Gianna, who dreamed of playing in the WNBA. In January 2020, Bryant and his daughter died in a helicopter crash. Ionescu dedicated the rest of her senior season to Kobe and Gianna.

CHAPTER FIVE

WNBA ROOKIE

On April 17, 2020, the New York Liberty selected the 22-year-old point guard with the number-one pick in the WNBA Draft. It was a difficult time to begin her career. COVID-19 changed everything. The WNBA pushed back the start of the season.

On July 25, Ionescu stepped onto the court for her first pro game. The long break may have had a bad effect on her skills. She shot 0–8 in her three-point attempts. She was 4–17 overall. The Liberty lost to the Seattle Storm, 87–71.

>>> Ionescu goes for a shot in her WNBA debut.

>>> During her debut WNBA game, Ionescu faced the Seattle Storm's star forward, Breanna Stewart (right).

Ionescu bounced back with a huge game four days later. She scored 33 points and added seven rebounds and seven assists. Then in her third pro game, Ionescu injured her ankle. The **rookie's** season was over after just two and a half games.

FUTURE STAR?

As the 2021 season began, the Liberty were off to a great start. In their first game on May 14, Ionescu sunk a three-point buzzer-beater to win the game over the Indiana Fever. She led her team to an early 4–1 record and was named Eastern Conference Player of the Week. On May 18, she became the youngest player in WNBA history to get a triple-double.

Many fans believe Ionescu will become one of the greatest to ever play in the WNBA. She is still young. It is too early to tell what kind of professional career Ionescu will have. But her fans in New York hope she stays healthy and brings a WNBA Championship to the Liberty!

〉〉〉 Ionescu reacts with excitement after making a game-winning basket in May 2021.

TIMELINE

1997 Sabrina Ionescu is born in Walnut Creek, California, on December 6.

2016 Ionescu is named the USA Today Girls Basketball Player of the Year.

2016 Ionescu wins the Gatorade State Player of the Year for California.

2017 Ionescu is named PAC-12 Freshman of the Year.

2019 Ionescu wins a gold medal as a member of the USA Basketball 3x3 team.

2020 Ionescu becomes the only player in NCAA history to score 2,000 points and have 1,000 assists and 1,000 rebounds in a college career.

2020 The New York Liberty select Ionescu with the number-one pick in the WNBA Draft on April 17.

2020 Ionescu makes her WNBA debut on July 25, scoring 12 points and collecting six rebounds.

GLOSSARY

COVID-19 (KO-vid NINE-teen)—a mild to severe respiratory illness that is caused by a coronavirus

MENTOR (MEN-tur)—a trusted adviser or teacher

PANDEMIC (pan-DEM-ik)—a disease that spreads over a wide area and affects many people

PLAYOFF GAME (PLAY-awf GAYM)—a game in a series played after the regular season to decide a championship

RECRUIT (ri-KROOT)—a person who is asked to join a team; colleges recruit players for their teams

ROOKIE (RUK-ee)—a first-year player

SCOUT (SKOWT)—someone who looks for players who might be good fits for a team

TRIPLE-DOUBLE (TRI-pul-DU-bul)—when a player gets a total of 10 or more points, assists, and rebounds in one game

READ MORE

Chandler, Matt. *On the Court: Biographies of Today's Best Basketball Players.* Emeryville, CA: Rockridge Press, 2020.

Frederick, Shane. *Candace Parker: Basketball Star.* North Mankato, MN: Capstone, 2020.

Jankowski, Matt. *The Greatest Basketball Players of All Time.* New York: Gareth Stevens Publishing, 2020.

INTERNET SITES

ESPN: The Legend of Sabrina Ionescu
espn.com/espn/feature/story/_/id/28878754/the-legend-sabrina-ionescu

WNBA: Sabrina Ionescu
wnba.com/player/sabrina-ionescu

WNBA's 25 Most Defining Milestones
espn.com/espn/feature/story/_/id/31270404/the-25-firsts-defined-wnba-25-years

Bright Idea Books are published by Capstone Press
1710 Roe Crest Drive, North Mankato, Minnesota 56003
www.mycapstone.com

Library of Congress Cataloging-in-Publication Data
Names: Chanez, Katie, author.
Title: Alien abductions / by Katie Chanez.
Description: North Mankato, Minnesota : Capstone Press, [2020] | Series:
  Aliens | Includes index. | Audience: Grade 4 to 6. Identifiers:
  LCCN 2018060987 (print) | LCCN 2019000500 (ebook) | ISBN
  9781543571110 (ebook) | ISBN 9781543571035 (hardcover) | ISBN   9781543574906 (pbk.)
Subjects: LCSH: Alien abduction--Juvenile literature. | Human-alien
  encounters--Juvenile literature.
Classification: LCC BF2050 (ebook) | LCC BF2050 .C463 2020 (print) | DDC 001.942--dc23
LC record available at https://lccn.loc.gov/2018060987

All internet sites appearing in back matter were available and accurate when this book was sent to press.

Editorial Credits
Editor: Claire Vanden Branden
Designer: Becky Daum
Production Specialist: Melissa Martin

Photo Credits
Alamy: AF archive/Paramount Pictures, 15, World History Archive, 9; iStockphoto: AntonioGuillem, 22–23, cosmin4000, 11, 28, goktugg, 31, gremlin, 24–25, Magnilion, 16–17, Mike_Kiev, cover, patrickheagney, 6–7; Shutterstock Images: Fer Gregory, 21, ktsdesign, 5, lassedesignen, 26–27, Linda Bucklin, 18–19, 29, vchal, 12–13

Design Elements: Shutterstock Images, Red Line Editorial

Printed in the United States of America.
PA70

OF CONTENTS

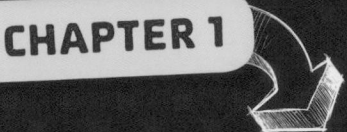

CHAPTER 1

TAKEN

Barney and Betty Hill were driving home in 1961. They had been on vacation. Suddenly a light appeared above them. The light chased their car. They kept driving. But the light kept following. Then they both fell asleep.

Barney and Betty woke up. They were miles away. They could not remember how they got there.

Barney and Betty Hill said they were taken by aliens on September 19, 1961.

People who are under hypnosis go into a trance. Many believe hypnosis can help access memories deep in their brains.

Betty started having dreams about that night. She dreamed aliens had stopped their car. The aliens brought them onto their spaceship. She could not get this out of her mind.

The Hills decided to see a doctor. The doctor suggested **hypnosis**. It could help them remember what happened to them.

The Hills decided to try it. Afterward they said aliens had **abducted** them. The aliens studied them. Then the aliens took them back to their car. They made Betty and Barney forget what happened.

THE UFO INCIDENT

A movie was made in 1975 about Barney and Betty's abduction. It was called *The UFO Incident*. Reports of alien abductions rose after the movie aired.

The Hills told many people their story.

CHAPTER 2

WHO ARE the Aliens?

Betty said the aliens had gray skin. They had big eyes. They also had small ears and noses. They were about 5 feet (1.5 meters) tall. Barney said they wore black clothes. Many believers call these aliens "Greys."

Believers think most Greys have large eyes and a big head.

GREYS

No one knows for sure if the Greys are real. They also don't know why the Greys take people. Most Greys seem friendly. They let the people go. Betty said one Grey even made a joke.

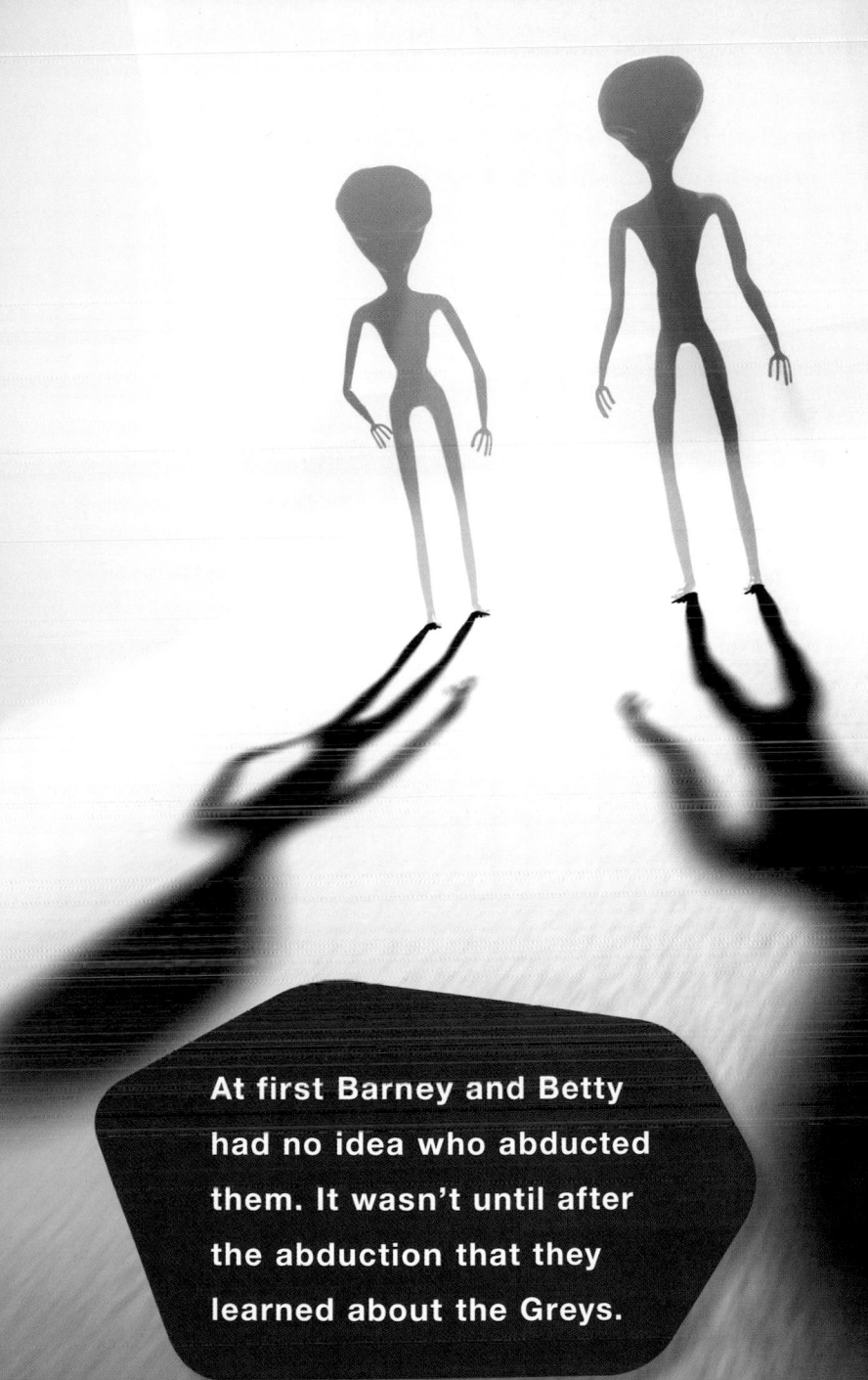

At first Barney and Betty had no idea who abducted them. It wasn't until after the abduction that they learned about the Greys.

NORDICS

The Greys are not the only aliens who are said to take people. Some people say there are aliens called Nordics. They look more like humans than Greys do. They are tall. Sometimes they have blond or red hair. They have been said to take people too.

A movie was made in 1993 about Travis Walton's story. It was called *Fire in the Sky*.

Travis Walton said aliens took him once. They could have been Nordics. He was working in Arizona. One night he and a few men were driving home. They saw a strange light in the sky.

Walton got out to look at it. The men say the light suddenly took Walton.

Walton showed up five days later. He said aliens took him. He woke up on the aliens' spaceship. He later wrote a book about what happened to him.

Walton said that he found the control room on the alien spaceship.

Some people say Reptilians look like lizards.

REPTILIANS

Some people say Reptilians have taken them. These are **shapeshifters**. They have heads like snakes. Most are very tall. They like to hurt people.

CHAPTER 3

ARE PEOPLE Really Taken?

Most scientists don't believe in alien abductions. They say people only think they are taken. This may be because of a sleep condition.

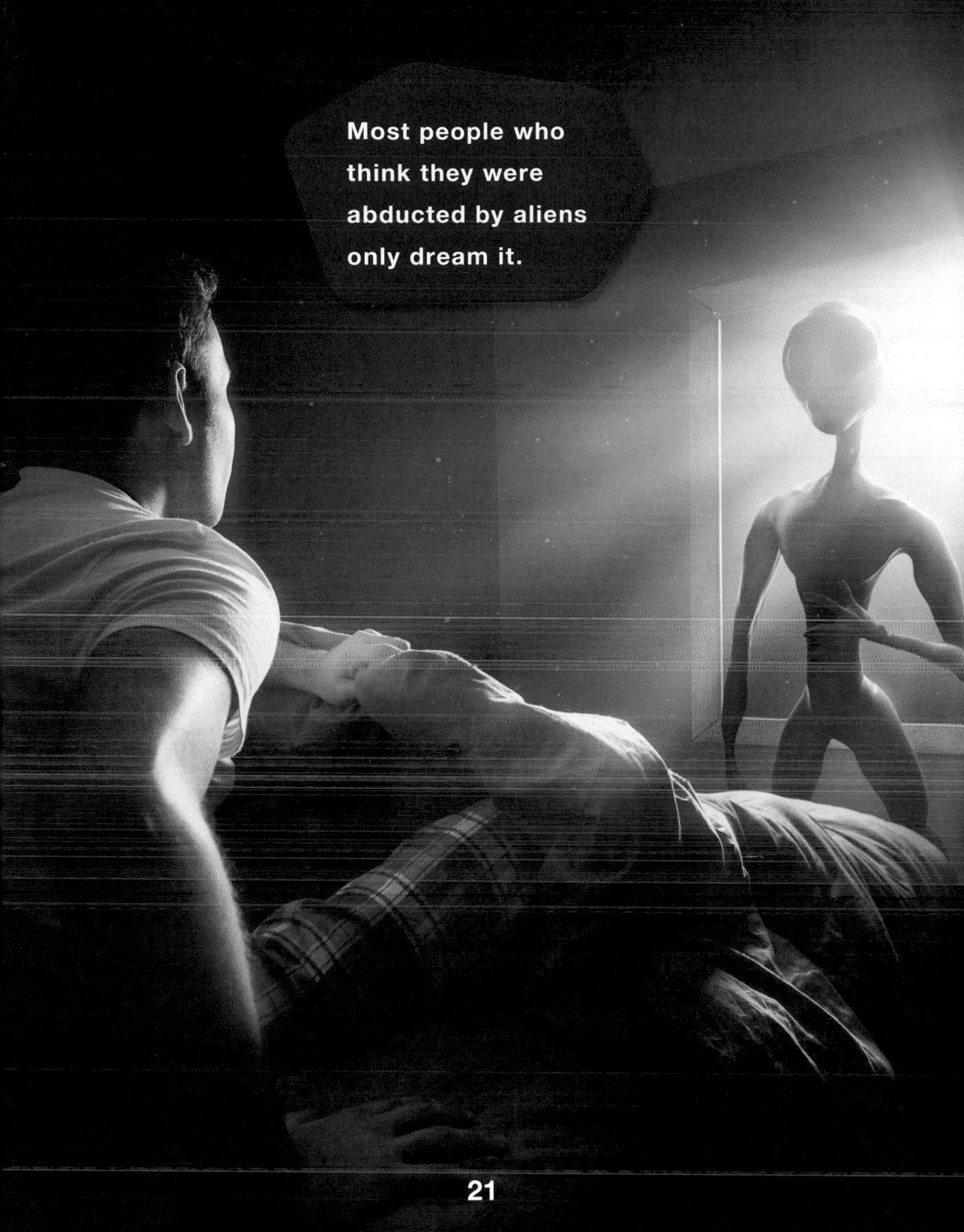

Most people who think they were abducted by aliens only dream it.

Your body relaxes when you fall asleep. Sometimes people wake up suddenly. They cannot move right away. It can be scary. Sometimes people think they see things that are not there. They are still dreaming.

A person experiencing sleep paralysis cannot move.

Many people who say they were taken do not remember it right away. People can remember things differently. **Hypnotists** can accidentally make people believe things. Sometimes people remember things that never happened.

GREYS ON TELEVISION

Many TV shows and movies show the Greys. One show was on almost two weeks before Barney used hypnosis. Some people think he remembered the TV show.

Hypnosis can sometimes make people think they saw things that never were there.

Most scientists think people have only imagined that they were taken by aliens.

Many people say aliens have taken them. Most scientists think there are other explanations. Believers think scientists are ignoring the truth.

GLOSSARY

abduct
to take a person by force

hypnosis
the process of putting
someone in a trancelike state

hypnotist
a person who puts someone
else under hypnosis

shapeshifter
a person or creature that
can change its physical form
or shape

TRIVIA

1. Betty Hill said the Greys showed her a star map, which she later drew.

2. Some people believe that government officials from around the world are secretly Reptilians, also called lizard people. They think Reptilians want to take over the world.

3. About 6 million Americans have reported being abducted by aliens.

ACTIVITY

CREATE YOUR OWN ALIENS!

Think about the different kinds of aliens mentioned in the book. Now come up with your own aliens. Where are they from? Do they abduct people? Why? What do they hope to do or learn? You can write a story from the point of view of the alien or the human. You could write one side of the story and have a friend write another.

31

FURTHER RESOURCES

Want to know more about alien abductions? Learn more here:

Martin, Michael. *The Unsolved Mystery of Alien Abductions.* Unexplained Mysteries. North Mankato, Minn.: Capstone Press, 2014.

Interested in learning more about aliens? Check out these resources:

Chanez, Katie. *UFO Sightings.* Aliens. North Mankato, Minn.: Capstone Press, 2020.

Hile, Lori. *Aliens and UFOs: Myth or Reality?* Investigating Unsolved Mysteries. North Mankato, Minn.: Capstone Press, 2019.

PBS Learning Media: Search for Extraterrestrial Intelligence: Are We Alone? https://tpt.pbslearningmedia.org/resource/ess05.sci.ess.eiu.alone/search-for-extraterrestrial-intelligence-are-we-alone

INDEX